CONTENTS

Extension Activities

OVERVIEW

Readers' Theater is a supplemental reading program designed to provide students with successful reading experiences. This collection of four high-interest plays will draw in even the most reluctant readers and provide them ample opportunities to build self-confidence through oral reading. The plays all revolve around adventures and are sure to engage students and hold their interest.

The National Council of Teachers of English proclaimed in a resolution requesting funding for workshops and experimental theater companies, "the conviction that live performances are the most effective way to help students comprehend and appreciate dramatic literature." Giving students the opportunity to participate in *Readers' Theater* is a fitting introduction to the pleasures of drama.

A VARIETY OF READING LEVELS

Almost every student will be able to participate comfortably because of the wide range of reading levels found in the plays. Each play has nine or ten characters. Reading levels for individual characters range from 2.0 to 6.6 as measured by the Spache and Dale-Chall readability formulas.

ORGANIZATION OF THE TEACHER'S GUIDE

The two- or three-page Teacher's Guide before each play provides easy-to-follow teaching suggestions for that play.

Meet the Players provides a list of characters, and identifies the readability levels for each. The list may be used to assign appropriate parts based on students' reading levels. You may wish to read the most difficult part when necessary. In small groups, you may wish to assign more than one character's part to several students.

Play Summary provides a brief summary of each play. You may use the summary to quickly become familiar with the plot of the play.

Vocabulary lists words in the play that are above the sixth-grade level. While some of these words may be familiar to students, their usage may not. You may wish to use these words in vocabulary activities before students read the play.

Tapping Prior Knowledge helps prepare and motivate students to read the play. Several questions are provided which elicit personal responses from students—responses that come from experiences and feelings they have had. The questions may be used to set the stage for the play.

Thinking It Over provides questions that can be used after students have read a play. The questions may be used to monitor students' comprehension of the play.

Presenting the Play provides suggestions for sound effects and props for presenting the play as a radio play and/or as a classroom play.

Supplementing the Play provides ideas for cross-curricular activities, including language arts, social studies, and writing. The activities may be used to enrich the students' reading of the play in individual, small, and large groups.

EXTENSION ACTIVITIES

The extension activities at the back of this book may be reproduced for use in the classroom or at home. The five activity masters are designed in such a way that any or all of them may be used upon completion of each play. Depending on students' abilities, you may wish to assign different activities to individual students. You may also wish to have students work cooperatively in pairs or in groups to complete the activities.

Studying the Elements of a Play asks students to complete sentences describing a play's characters, setting, and plot.

Comparing Characters is a chart on which students describe two characters' personality traits. Students are then asked to write a paragraph comparing the two characters.

Understanding the Characters encourages students to describe characters in a play based on characters' dialogue and actions.

Making a Play Map is a means by which students tell what happens in a play.

Choosing an Alternate Ending challenges students to write a new ending for a play.

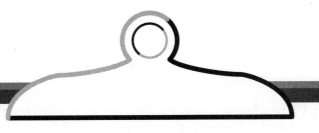

Dear Parent,

Whether presenting a report at work or reading a bedtime story to a child, oral reading is a skill we use throughout life. Being able to read clearly and with expression brings pleasure to both the reader and the listener. This year our class will be reading parts in plays in order to increase oral reading ability and to allow students to experience the fun of participating in a play.

Using *Readers' Theater*, we will be performing several plays in our class. Students will be assigned parts at their approximate reading level, and may bring home a play to practice. You can help by listening to your child read his or her part and providing encouragement.

From time to time, I may send home an activity sheet or a project related to the play we are reading. These activities are designed to enrich students' understanding of the play. To best help your child, please consider the following suggestions:

- Provide a quiet place to work.
- Read the directions together.
- Listen to your child's ideas.
- Check the lesson when it is complete.

You may also want to check out a book of plays from the library to read with your child. Watching a play on television, or better yet, attending a live performance would be a wonderful way for you to share this form of entertainment with your child. Suggest that your child and his or her friends make up a play and perform it for you.

Thank you for your help!

Cordially,

MEET THE PLAYERS

Character	Reading Level
Narrator	5.1
Josie Chang, *a twin*	4.8
Jay Chang, *a twin*	4.5
Sergeant Lucy Chang, *the twins' mother*	5.0
Uncle Charley, *the twins' uncle*	2.4
James Porch, *the twins' friend*	2.2
Paula Sharpe, *the twins' friend*	3.0
Mrs. Gonzales, *a teacher*	2.0
Bank Robber	3.9

PLAY SUMMARY

Twins Josie and Jay Chang accidentally come into contact with some liquid in their uncle's laboratory that makes them invisible. This event complicates their lives, both with their friends and in school. They go to their mother, a police officer, for help. Outside police headquarters they learn a robber is holding hostages inside a bank. Using their invisibility, the twins slip into the bank and so confuse the robber that he meekly surrenders. The effects of the liquid do wear off, and the twins return to normal.

VOCABULARY

While the character parts of *The Disappearing Changs* are written to accommodate a variety of reading levels, you may wish to use the following words in vocabulary activities.

point, p. 14	*leave,* p. 24
yet, p. 16	*meekly,* p. 24

TAPPING PRIOR KNOWLEDGE

Before reading *The Disappearing Changs,* you may wish to discuss the following questions with students.

1. What good things could you do if you were invisible? What might be dangerous about being invisible?

2. In which ways might your life change if you were invisible? Think about ordinary events, such as visiting a friend, going shopping, or going to school.

THINKING IT OVER

The following questions may be used in a variety of ways after students read *The Disappearing Changs*. Each question may be discussed orally as a class or in small groups, or it may be answered as part of a written classroom or home-work assignment.

1. Why didn't the twins' mother want them to take care of their uncle's pets? Why did she finally agree to let them do so?

2. How did the twins react to being invisible? Did they enjoy the experience or not? Explain your answer.

3. Describe how the twins used being invisible to good advantage.

PRESENTING THE PLAY

Radio Play

The following sound effects will help you present *The Disappearing Changs* as a radio play.

- taped music to indicate act breaks — pp. 9, 10, 12, 13, 15, 17, 18, 22, 23, 24
- school bell — Act Four, p. 13; Act Six, p. 17
- trash can crashing — Act Four, p. 15
- teenagers' voices — Act Six, p. 17
- door opening and closing — Act Seven, pp. 19, 22

Classroom Play

All the sound effects listed for the radio play can also be used to stage the play in the classroom. Additionally, you may wish to use the props listed below.

- bottle — Act Two, pp. 10–11
- mop — Act Two, p. 11
- trash can — Act Four, p. 15
- bicycles — Act Five, p. 15; Act Six, pp. 17–18; Act Seven, p. 18; Act Eight, p. 23
- cap pistol — Act Seven, pp. 20–22
- play money — Act Seven, pp. 19–22

EXTENDING THE PLAY

You may wish to use some of the following activities to enrich the students' reading of *The Disappearing Changs*.

1. The blackline masters included in this Teacher's Guide can be duplicated for use with any of the *Readers' Theater* plays.

2. Tell students to imagine they are Jay or Josie Chang. Have them write a letter to a friend describing how it feels to be invisible.

3. Have students design a plaque to be awarded the Chang twins for persuading the bank robber to give up.

The Disappearing Changs

by Laurence Swinburne

Cast
(in order of appearance)

Narrator

Uncle Charley, *the twins' uncle*

Josie Chang ⎫
⎬ *twins*
Jay Chang ⎭

Sergeant Lucy Chang, *the twins' mother*

James Porch ⎫
⎬ *the twins' friends*
Paula Sharpe ⎭

Mrs. Gonzales, *a teacher*

Bank Robber

Readers' Theater, SV 6175-3

Act One

Narrator: You remember the Chang twins, Jay and Josie? Their mother, Lucy Chang, is a police sergeant, and their father is an officer in the navy. Well, even if you don't know them, I should tell you the neighborhood never remains calm very long if the twins have anything to say about it. And they usually do. Take the time they got involved with their Uncle Charley. It started innocently enough. Uncle Charley, who lives just down the street from the Changs, asked for a small favor. How could anything go wrong?

Uncle Charley: Look, kids, I've got to go to Boston on business tonight. I'll be back late tomorrow afternoon. Will you feed Rex and Meow for me while I'm gone?

Josie: Sure, Uncle Charley.

Jay: No problem.

Uncle Charley: You'll find pet food in the refrigerator. Feed Meow a pound of hamburger meat. Give Rex half of one of the small cans of tuna. Can you feed them in the morning before you go to school and let them out in the back yard? After school you can bring them back into the house.

Jay: We'll do it.

Uncle Charley: Thanks. *(Pauses)* There's one more thing. Don't go near my laboratory. *(Whispering)* You see, I'm working on a marvelous invention. It's not completed yet, so it could be dangerous.

Jay: Don't worry, Uncle Charley. We won't go near the lab.

Josie: We positively will not.

Uncle Charley: Thanks, kids. I know I can trust you.

Narrator: Lucy Chang isn't so sure about Jay and Josie helping her brother, though. They tell her the news as soon as she comes home from her shift at police headquarters.

Sergeant Chang: Oh, I don't know, kids. Charley may be my brother, but he's a strange one when it comes to his experiments. Remember the time he almost blew up his house?

Josie: Mom, we did promise not to go near his lab.

Sergeant Chang: I do love Charley; but he is odd. Imagine having a tiny cat called Rex and naming a monster of a dog Meow. That takes a weird sense of humor.

Jay: Mom, you're not being fair. I think Dad should be in on the decision. Why don't we call him? I bet he'd say it's okay.

Sergeant Chang: You know perfectly well he's at sea, and I can't reach him. *(Pauses)* Maybe I am making too much of this. All right, do what Charley wants. Please be careful, though.

Act Two

Narrator: So the twins go to Uncle Charley's house the next morning.

Josie: Rex!

Jay: Meow!

Narrator: Meow, a huge Great Dane, comes running towards them. He puts his front paws on Josie's shoulders.

Josie: *(Laughing)* Stop that, Meow! You'll get my blouse all dirty!

Jay: Where's Rex? She's always with Meow.

Josie: Oh, she's around somewhere. Come on. Let's get their food. I don't want to be late for school.

Narrator: Jay and Josie lead Meow down the hall to the kitchen at the rear of the house.

Josie: *(Gasping)* Look, Jay, the door to Uncle Charley's lab is open!

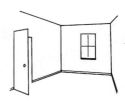

Jay: He probably was in a hurry and forgot to lock it. I'll just close it and…

Josie: *(Looking into the lab)* The lab's a mess. The animals must have gotten in.

Jay: You know Uncle Charley isn't the neatest person around.

Josie: *(Pointing at the floor)* He never leaves anything spilled on the floor. We better clean it up before we go.

Jay: Well, okay. I'm beginning to wish we hadn't agreed to take care of Uncle Charley's pets.

Narrator: Jay begins straightening out lab equipment on the table while Josie mops the floor. Josie carries the wet mop to the sink to rinse it out.

Jay: Watch out, Josie. You just got me all wet.

Josie: Sorry, Jay. I got some on me, too. It shouldn't hurt anything. It feels like water.

Jay: Water? It looks as if it came from the big container labeled "Experiment 101" that was by the spill. It might be some kind of acid for all we know.

Josie: I doubt that. My hands aren't burning. I don't think it's anything to worry about.

Narrator: The twins leave the laboratory, closing the door tightly behind them. They walk down the hall to the kitchen with Meow behind them. They get out the pet food and fill the bowls.

Jay: I wish I knew where Rex was.

Josie: I thought I heard her a few minutes ago. She must be around somewhere. Open the back door so they can run around the yard. *(Looking at her watch)* We better hurry, or we'll be late for school.

Jay: I'll be right with you, Josie. I think I saw her tail over there by the refrigerator.

Josie: *(Giggling)* All you see is her tail? Where's the rest of her?

Jay: I don't know. Her tail was just floating in the air.

Josie: Mom always says you have some kind of imagination. A floating tail! What will you see next?

Act Three

Narrator: It isn't only Jay who is—or is not—seeing things. Later, Jay and Josie are standing outside the school with two of their friends, waiting for the bell to ring.

James: I've got to get new glasses.

Jay: You just got new glasses last month, didn't you, James? You said they were fine then.

James: They were. But when I looked at you just now, you seemed to disappear. Then you came right back. It was like turning the TV off and on.

Jay:	Now, James, you don't really think…
James:	*(Excitedly)* It happened again! How do you do that, Jay?
Paula:	James and Jay, watch Josie because she is also disappearing and reappearing!
James:	That's a great trick! Let us in on the secret.
Josie:	You're kidding, right? You made this up before we got here. We really haven't disappeared. Have we?
James:	It's not a joke. You really…

Act Four

Narrator:	The school bell rings, ending the conversation. Everyone rushes into the school. The teenagers go to their lockers and then to Mrs. Gonzales's class. Once in the classroom, the students begin to settle down when…
Jay:	*(Whispering)* Josie, they're right! You just disappeared, and then you reappeared!
Josie:	*(Whispering)* You don't have to join in their jokes.
Jay:	*(Whispering)* I'm not. I'm telling the truth, Josie. I…
Josie:	*(Shocked)* You did it, too! Poof! You were gone! Then you were back again!
Mrs. Gonzales:	Well, Josie and Jay, is there something going on that I should know? Or may I start our lesson about water?
Josie:	My brother and I—well, it's nothing. *(Pauses)* I'm sorry, Mrs. Gonzales.
Jay:	*(Whispering)* What should we do, Josie?

Josie:	*(Whispering)* I don't know.
Mrs. Gonzales:	Josie—Josie Chang—answer the question, please.
Josie:	I'm sorry, Mrs. Gonzales. Could you repeat that?
Mrs. Gonzales:	I don't know what's wrong with you kids today. It must be spring. *(Pauses)* Well, Josie, I asked you what happens to water when it is heated to the boiling point.
Josie:	It changes to water vapor, or steam, Mrs. Gonzales.
Mrs. Gonzales:	Very good. In other words, it disappears. *(Looking surprised)* It disappears just like your brother, Josie. Where has he gone?
Josie:	I...I think he must be around here—somewhere.
Jay:	*(Whispering)* I must have vanished again, Josie!
Josie:	*(Whispering)* You did. Only this time you didn't reappear!
Mrs. Gonzales:	*(Angrily)* I believe I hear Mr. Chang. Young man, if you do not appear in your seat immediately, you will have to answer to me!
Jay:	*(Whispering)* I'm in my seat. How do I reappear?
Josie:	*(Whispering)* I'll ask to leave the room. You sneak out behind me. We've got to get out of here so we can think of something.
Mrs. Gonzales:	*(Angrily)* I've had about as much of this as I'm going to take. Mr. Chang, where are you? Miss Chang, do you know where your brother is?

14

Narrator: Josie rises from her seat. As she does, she begins to fade out, until only her hand is visible. She raises her hand and is about to speak when she notices the color leave Mrs. Gonzales's face. Mrs. Gonzales sinks into her chair. Her mouth is open, but she is unable to speak.

Josie: *(Whispering)* Come on, Jay. Let's go!

Narrator: As the twins run for the door, Jay trips over James's feet. Jay falls to the floor with a crash, knocking over a trash can. Mrs. Gonzales stares wide-eyed.

Mrs. Gonzales: This is amazing—very amazing!

Jay: *(Whispering)* Keep your big feet under your desk, James!

James: *(Whispering)* How do you do it, Jay? I can't see you at all.

Jay: *(Whispering)* I wish I knew. Look, I've got to get out of here. See you later.

James: *(Whispering)* I hope I can see you later!

Narrator: Once he gets to the hall, Jay calls out.

Jay: Josie, where are you?

Josie: I'm over here, Jay. I think we better hold hands. Otherwise, we'll lose each other.

Jay: Where are we going?

Josie: We'll go to Uncle Charley's, of course. Come on. Let's get our bikes.

Act Five

Narrator: People stare at the two bicycles that appear to be moving by themselves. Finally, the twins arrive at Uncle Charley's. Meow runs up to Josie and begins to lick her invisible face.

Jay: He knows you! That's a good sign.

Josie: He's the only one that does, so far. Look! There's the tip of Rex's tail. It's floating in the air!

Jay: I told you I saw a tail this morning. Come on. We better get to the lab to see what we can find to get us out of this mess.

Narrator: In the laboratory, the twins search for a clue. Then…

Jay: *(Excitedly)* Here are Uncle Charley's lab notes!

Josie: What do they say? Is there anything there that might help us?

Jay: *(Reading)* April 10. At last! I have found a way to make objects invisible to the human eye. I dipped several pencils into the liquid I call "Experiment 101." Within minutes, they vanished. Yet, I can still feel them. As a matter of fact, I am writing these notes with an invisible pencil.

Josie: This is of no help. We already know he can make objects vanish. Look at us. Give me the notes. *(She takes them and begins to read.)* April 11. I sprinkled some of the liquid on a frog today, and now it has vanished. Amazingly, the pencils are still invisible.

Jay: That means…

Josie: *(Sadly)* Yes, it means no one may ever see us again!

Jay: Well. I'm not giving up. There has to be a way. *(Pauses)* I know! Let's do what we always do whenever we get into too much trouble.

Josie: Go to Mom?

Jay: That's right. She'll know what to do.

Josie: That may not be too easy to do. Remember, people can't see us, but they can see the bikes. If we ride downtown to police headquarters, we'll cause an uproar or a riot! We'd never get to Mom.

Jay: I know how we can do it. We'll get our friends to help!

Act Six

Narrator: The twins take side streets and back alleys to the school, where they wait for the final bell of the day. Students come running out of the building to the bicycle rack where the twins are waiting. Jay grabs James's arm and scares him.

Jay: Take it easy, James. It's only me…Jay.

James: Take it easy? How can I? I'm not used to talking to an invisible person, you know.

Josie: Listen. We have to get downtown to police headquarters. Maybe our mom can help us get out of this mess.

James: This may be the one time she won't be able to help—unless she's a miracle worker. *(Pauses)* What do you want me to do?

Jay: Get Paula. The two of you will ride on either side of us. Maybe nobody will notice our bikes.

James:	I wouldn't bet on that, but I'll do it.
Narrator:	James finds Paula. They put their bikes on either side of Jay's and Josie's.
Paula:	This is truly an amazing adventure, but what we are doing now is really crazy!
James:	Why's that, Paula?
Paula:	We're trying to hide people who are invisible!
Josie:	Come on! We're wasting time!

Act Seven

Narrator:	The plan works, and the twins reach police headquarters without causing any trouble.
Jay:	Thanks a lot. We'll see you later.
Paula:	Now that is nonsense! We took the time to bring you here, and we'll see this plan through to the end.
James:	Paula's right. We're curious to see how your mom will get you out of this mess. We don't think she can. (*Chuckling*) Maybe she'll just throw a bucket of paint over the two of you. She'll be able to see you then!
Narrator:	The twins and their friends are nearly run over by Sergeant Chang, who is dashing out of the police station.
Josie:	Mom! Oh, Mom!
Sergeant Chang:	I can't talk now, Josie. This is an emergency. The bank around the corner has just been robbed, and I've got to get over there!
Jay:	Come on, Josie. Let's follow Mom.

Readers' Theater, SV 6175-3

Josie: She'll be so angry if she finds us over there. You know she doesn't want us around when she's on a dangerous job.

Jay: How's she going to know? No one can see us. Besides, she didn't notice you weren't there when you called her name.

Josie: Well, okay, then. Maybe we can help somehow.

Narrator: The invisible twins run around the corner to the bank, which is surrounded by police. Sergeant Chang is giving the orders.

Sergeant Chang: Listen. There's one robber in there. He's armed, and he's holding two tellers as hostages. I don't want any shots fired unless I give the order. That means no shooting! Does everyone understand?

Jay: *(Whispering)* Come on, Josie. We're going inside the bank.

Josie: *(Whispering)* Are you crazy?

Jay: *(Whispering)* Of course not, Josie. Remember, no one can see us. We'll slip inside and see what's going on. Then we'll slip back out and tell Mom.

Josie: *(Whispering)* Now, that's a good idea. Let's hold hands so we don't lose each other.

Narrator: The invisible twins slip through the police lines and quietly enter the bank through a side door. Inside, the bank robber paces nervously back and forth. He holds a gun in one hand. Several bags of money are lying scattered on the floor. Money is lying everywhere. The hostages are nowhere in sight.

Readers' Theater, SV 6175-3

Bank Robber:	*(Aloud)* What have I done? I'm in a terrible mess. Why did I think I could get away with robbing a bank? What do I do now?
Jay:	Where are the hostages?
Bank Robber:	What's going on here? Who said that?
Josie:	He said, "Where are the hostages?"
Bank Robber:	*(Waving his gun)* Look, you better show yourselves! I will shoot!
Jay:	Shoot if you will. Who are you going to hit? You can't see us. We're invisible.
Josie:	We are real, though. Now where are the hostages?
Bank Robber:	*(Nervously)* Am I going crazy or what? *(Pauses)* Okay, so I can't see you. That doesn't mean I won't shoot. Someone will get hit!
Jay:	You would shoot the hostages?
Bank Robber:	No, I won't shoot them. They're okay. They're locked in the office. They may be a bit scared.
Josie:	Like you?
Bank Robber:	*(Trying to sound tough)* Who are you calling scared? I know what I'm doing. Anyone who gets in my way had better…had better…
Jay:	That person had better what?
Bank Robber:	He or she had better watch out! That's what! *(Pauses)* Besides, how do I know you're really here? Why can't I see you?
Narrator:	Without answering, Jay slips up behind the bank robber. He taps him on the shoulder,

Readers' Theater, SV 6175-3

then he quickly steps aside. The bank robber swings around, pointing his gun.

Jay: I'm not there anymore! I'm over here!

Narrator: The bank robber swings around again. As he does, Josie slips up behind him and taps him on the other shoulder.

Josie: I've got you!

Bank Robber: *(Angrily)* Look, you two—whoever you are…or whatever you are.

Jay: Why don't you shoot? Why?

Bank Robber: Oh, what's the use? How can I fight what I can't see? I don't know what's going on, but I've had enough. *(Holding his gun out)* Here, take this. It's not real. It's a cap pistol.

Josie: It looked real to me.

Jay: You sure don't act like a bank robber. You're not like the ones our mom talks about.

Bank Robber: *(Sadly)* I'm not. This was my first try. It looks like my last, too. I lost my money in a bank that failed. My whole life's savings are gone! Bill collectors are calling about my house and my car. I have other bills to pay, too. The place where I work is going out of business. It's all gotten to me. So, I decided to get some money this way. Then I could start over in a different place. *(Laughs)* That wasn't such a good idea, was it? *(Pauses)* By the way, who is your mother? Why does she tell you about bank robbers?

Josie: She's a police officer. In fact, she's outside. Sergeant Chang is her name.

Jay:	I bet if you just walked to the door and called her name, she'd let you go out.
Bank Robber:	*(Sighing)* Well, I guess I should give up. I can't see any other way out of this mess.
Josie:	Even if there were another way, this is the right way. I don't know what good it'll do, but we'll talk to our mom about you.
Jay:	We'll tell her about your problems.
Bank Robber:	Thanks. Let the tellers go, please. The key is by the door. I wasn't going to hurt them.
Narrator:	Slowly, the bank robber steps to the main entrance of the bank and calls out.
Bank Robber:	I'm coming out, Sergeant Chang. My hands are up. I don't have a gun.
Narrator:	Sergeant Chang sends the bank robber to headquarters with the other police officers. She stays behind to calm down a little.

Act Eight

Narrator:	While Sergeant Chang is alone, or so she thinks, she takes several deep breaths to relax.
Sergeant Chang:	I'm glad that's over. I wonder why he changed his mind.
Josie:	*(Softly)* Mom?
Sergeant Chang:	Who's that?
Jay:	It's us, Mom. It's your kids—Josie and Jay.
Sergeant Chang:	*(Looking around)* Where are you? I don't see anyone. Oh, I know. It's a joke. You're talking through a microphone. Where's the speaker?

Josie: There is no microphone or speaker, Mom. *(Pauses)* Just listen, Mom. Jay and I are invisible. This morning we had to clean up Uncle Charley's lab and…

Sergeant Chang: *(Interrupting)* Charley! That brother of mine! I should have known! So you're invisible, are you? Well, if Charley's mixed up in this, then I believe you. Now, don't say another word. I've got to get you home.

Narrator: The twins follow their mother to the police station. They are careful not to bump into anyone. Outside, standing on the sidewalk, the twins' friends are still waiting.

Paula: Where are Josie and Jay, Mrs. Chang?

Sergeant Chang: Do you kids know what happened to them?

James: Yes, Mrs. Chang. They're invisible.

Paula: We came to the police station with them.

Sergeant Chang: You've been very helpful. The twins, who are beside me, will tell you all about their adventure tomorrow. *(Pauses)* I see their bikes. Will you put them in the trunk of my car, please?

Josie: Thanks, Paula and James.

Jay: We couldn't have done a thing without you.

Act Nine

Narrator: On the way home, the twins tell their mother about the events of the day. Sergeant Chang is silent until they get home.

Sergeant Chang: Well, I know that what happened is not your fault. The only mistake you made was

in agreeing to help your Uncle Charley.
Now we've got to find a way to make you
visible again. Your father will be home on
leave next week, and I'm sure he'd like to
see his children.

Narrator: Just then Uncle Charley bursts into the
room.

Uncle Charley: Where are those kids, Lucy? I told them not
to go into my lab, and what did I find? I
discovered they did. Honestly, I can't go
away for one night without...

Sergeant Chang: *(Interrupting)* Now just hold everything,
Charles.

Narrator: Furiously, Lucy Chang tells her brother
what has happened.

Uncle Charley: *(Meekly)* Well, I'm sorry, Lucy. I...I guess I
owe the twins an apology. You said they're
here?

Josie: We're right here, Uncle Charley.

Uncle Charley: I'm really sorry, kids.

Sergeant Chang: *(Angrily)* What will you do now, dear
brother?

Uncle Charley: Just calm down, Lucy. The stuff wears off in
a day or so. Josie and Jay will be as good as
new—you'll see.

Sergeant Chang: I'd better see.

Act Ten

Narrator: After dinner, the twins begin to reappear,
slowly. First Jay's legs reappear, and then
Josie's head reappears. By bedtime, the
twins are almost back to normal.

Sergeant Chang: *(Saying good night to the twins)* Well, one good thing came out of this mess. You two stopped a bank robbery. *(Pauses)* I'll get credit for that, of course. Although it isn't really fair. I'd love to tell everyone what really happened inside the bank. Who would believe me?

Josie: *(Giggling)* I would, Mom. Good night.

Jay: I'd believe you, too, Mom. Good night.

 Readers' Theater, SV 6175-3

MEET THE PLAYERS

Character	Reading Level
Narrator	5.8
Charlie Littlemoon, *a student in Mr. Nichols's class*	4.3
Mr. Nichols, *a school teacher*	5.1
Darryl Duckworth, *a student in Mr. Nichols's class*	4.3
Sylvia Acosta, *a student in Mr. Nichols's class*	2.0
Maxine Kaplan, *a student in Mr. Nichols's class*	2.3
Susan Ono, *a student in Mr. Nichols's class*	4.3
Rosalie Young, *a school bus driver*	2.3
Rob Grant, *a truck driver*	2.4
Walter Littlemoon, *Charlie's grandfather*	3.2

PLAY SUMMARY

David Nichols, a teacher, arranges a field trip for his class as part of a social studies unit on Native Americans. Mr. Nichols and his class travel by school bus onto the plains. One of the students, a Dakota Sioux named Charlie Littlemoon, talks to his classmates for several hours about what life was like on the plains one hundred years ago. As Charlie relates the stories his grandfather told him, a blizzard roars in, trapping everyone on the bus for the night. Everyone worries that the rescuers won't be able to find them. Then Charlie uses the old ways of the Sioux to find the rescue party and lead it to the stranded bus.

VOCABULARY

While the character parts of *The Field Trip* are written to accommodate a variety of reading levels, you may wish to use the following words in vocabulary activities.

matter, p. 31
mere, p. 31
portentous, pp. 31, 33, 35
awesome, p. 32
quite, pp. 32, 33
self-important, p. 33
style, p. 33
superb, p. 33

applicable, p. 34
mind, pp. 35, 38
newly, p. 35
pass, pp. 35, 36
bewildered, p. 35
runs, p. 36
features, p. 36
spot, p. 39

department, p. 41
goners, p. 42
out of the question, p. 42
start, pp. 43, 44
blankly, p. 44
mounted, p. 44

TAPPING PRIOR KNOWLEDGE

Before reading *The Field Trip,* you may wish to discuss the following questions with students.

1. Did any of your relatives or ancestors come from another country? If so, what do you know about their way of life in that country?

2. Do you think it is useful to learn about other cultures? Why or why not?

3. How does our understanding of the past affect what we do in the present and the future?

4. What movies, TV shows, or books have you seen or read recently about Native Americans? Do you think they told what life was really like for these people? Explain your answer.

5. If you could be transported back in time, what year would you choose? Explain your choice.

THINKING IT OVER

The following questions may be used in a variety of ways after students read *The Field Trip*. Each question may be discussed orally as a class or in small groups, or it may be answered as part of a written classroom or homework assignment.

1. When the play begins, what decision are the students trying to make? Why is this important?

2. Describe what kind of teacher Mr. Nichols is. Would you have liked to be in his classroom? Explain your answer.

3. How did Mr. Nichols get students interested in learning new vocabulary words? Do you think this was a better approach than just writing new vocabulary words on the chalkboard? Explain your answer.

4. Why does Charlie know so many stories about the Sioux?

5. Why was Charlie willing to be "teacher for a day" on the field trip?

6. Why doesn't Rosalie drive the bus back to the school? Do you think she made the right decision? Explain why or why not.

7. How does Mr. Nichols reassure the students that they will be all right spending the night on the bus?

8. Why did Charlie disobey Mr. Nichols and leave the bus before sunrise? Did he make the right choice? How did Mr. Nichols react to the news that Charlie had left the bus?

9. Why is Walter Littlemoon so proud of his grandson, Charlie, at the end of the play?

10. How does Charlie show that we can learn from history?

PRESENTING THE PLAY

Radio Play

The following sound effects will help you present *The Field Trip* as a radio play.

- taped music to indicate act breaks — pp. 31, 39, 43
- school bell — Act One, p. 31
- school bus engine — Act Two, p. 39; Act Three, pp. 43–47
- roaring wind — Act Two, pp. 40–42
- snowplow engine — Act Three, pp. 44–47

Classroom Play

All the sound effects listed for the radio play can also be used to stage the play in the classroom. Additionally, you may wish to use the props listed below.

- chairs and desk for classroom — Act One, pp. 31–38
- chalk and chalkboard — Act One, p. 34
- late pass — Act One, p. 36
- papers for permission slips — Act One, p. 38
- snowshoes, bow and arrows, pouch — Act Two, p. 39
- chairs arranged as school bus seats — Act Two, pp. 39–42; Act Three, pp. 43–47
- blankets — Act Two, p. 42

EXTENDING THE PLAY

You may wish to use some of the following activities to enrich the students' reading of *The Field Trip*.

1. The blackline masters included in this Teacher's Guide can be duplicated for use with any of the *Readers' Theater* plays.

2. Tell students to imagine they are Charlie Littlemoon. Have them write a note to Mr. Nichols telling him why Charlie left the bus to go for help.

3. Have students research the Sioux. Have them report on such things as housing, food, games, and other aspects of this Native American culture.

4. Have students research the Native American tribes that live (or lived) in their area. Ask students to present their findings in oral reports.

5. Tell students to imagine they are Darryl Duckworth. Have them write a diary entry describing the night of the blizzard.

6. Have students write a poem to express the way Charlie feels about his grandfather.

7. Have students imagine that they are Walter Littlemoon. Tell them to write a speech explaining why it is important to remember the old ways of the Sioux.

8. Have students make a list of the things they think were important to the Sioux one hundred years ago.

The Field Trip

by Jack Warner

Cast
(in order of appearance)

Narrator

Mr. Nichols, *a schoolteacher*

Darryl Duckworth

Sylvia Acosta

Maxine Kaplan   *students in Mr. Nichols's class*

Susan Ono

Charlie Littlemoon

Rosalie Young, *a school bus driver*

Rob Grant, *a truck driver*

Walter Littlemoon, *Charlie's grandfather*

       Readers' Theater, SV 6175-3

Act One

Narrator:	Eighth-grade teacher David Nichols is a favorite of all the students at the White River School. His classes are lively and interesting. His students help make important decisions, such as when to schedule tests and what field trips to take. One field trip that a class took in early February will be remembered for a long time.
Mr. Nichols:	*(After the school bell stops ringing)* Okay, that's it. Another day begins. Let's see. Where were we? Oh, now I remember. We were going to set a date for the unit test.
Darryl:	*(Groaning)* Do we have to, Mr. Nichols? I mean do we have to decide right at the start of class?
Sylvia:	It'll put us all in a bad mood, Mr. Nichols.
Maxine:	It'll positively ruin the whole day.
Mr. Nichols:	Well, it's got to be done soon. We can't ignore the test.
Susan:	I vote to talk about it later.
Mr. Nichols:	Vote? Did I hear you say vote, Susan? *(Looking around the room)* Since when have any of you been allowed to vote on a matter of such grave importance? Why, the mere thought of it is absolutely portentous, to say the least.

Susan: *(Giggling)* Mr. Nichols, you know you let us have a say in when to have tests and things. Besides, whenever you use big words, I know you're not all that serious.

Mr. Nichols: I'm using big words? What big words did I say? Darryl, did you hear any big words from me?

Darryl: Well, I think I did. There was one word I never heard before—*por...por...*

Susan: *...tentous. (Pronouncing it)* Por-TENT-us. That was the word.

Mr. Nichols: I see; and does anyone know what *portentous* means? Sylvia, do you?

Sylvia: Not really, Mr. Nichols. But the way you used it, it sure sounds heavy.

Mr. Nichols: You mean heavy as in bulky or hefty?

Sylvia: No, nothing like that.

Darryl: Heavy as in awesome, Mr. Nichols.

Mr. Nichols: *(Chuckling)* That's closer to being correct, Darryl, but not quite right. How about you, Maxine?

Maxine: Sorry, Mr. Nichols, I haven't the faintest idea what the word means. *(Pauses)* But I bet you're going to tell us real soon.

Mr. Nichols: *(Still chuckling)* Maxine, it looks as if I'll have to work up a new routine. You have me figured out. Actually, *portentous* has several meanings. One is "self-important." Listen to this example. "The author's style is portentous, but what she has to say is of little value."

Dictionary

Maxine: *(Laughing)* Sounds like Darryl, if you ask me.

Darryl: Good thing I can take a joke, Maxine. Besides, no one was asking you.

Susan: What are the other meanings, Mr. Nichols?

Mr. Nichols: I'm so glad you asked, Susan. A second meaning is "remarkable" or "superb."

Darryl: I've got a sentence for that, Mr. Nichols.

Mr. Nichols: Go ahead, Darryl. Give us an example.

Darryl: *(Clearing his throat)* "Maxine Kaplan does not tell portentous jokes!"

Mr. Nichols: That's not quite right, Darryl. But thanks for the effort. Listen to this example. "Darryl Duckworth is a student of portentous talent."

Darryl: *(Smiling broadly)* Much better, Mr. Nichols. In fact, that's perfect!

Sylvia: Now who's kidding, Mr. Nichols?

Mr. Nichols: And the third meaning, the one most applicable to my original use is, "alarming" or "frightening." Okay? *(Going to the chalkboard)* Let me write each of those meanings. We'll leave them here for a few days. They just might sink in.

Narrator: Caught up in the playful discussion, no one notices that the rear classroom door opens and Charlie Littlemoon slips quietly into his seat in the back row.

Susan: So, Mr. Nichols, do we get to vote on when to take the test?

Mr. Nichols: Oh, I suppose we shouldn't waste a vote on anything like that, Susan. *(Looking at his watch)* Why don't we talk about that five minutes before class ends?

Susan: That's great.

Mr. Nichols: And the rest of you—do you agree to put off the decision until then?

Students: *(Together)* Sure thing, Mr. Nichols.

Narrator: From the back of the room comes a near whisper, directed to Maxine Kaplan, but heard by everyone.

Charlie: Vote on what, Maxine?

Mr. Nichols: *(Looking up)* Oh, Master Littlemoon has arrived. Did you miss the bus, Charlie?

Charlie: Yes, sir. Then my grandfather had to drive me to school. He had to open his office at the museum first. That's why I'm late.

Darryl: A portentous excuse, Charlie, if I do say so.

Charlie: A what, Darryl?

Mr. Nichols: Don't mind Darryl, Charlie. He's just showing off his newly discovered way with words. I'm sure if we ignore him, he'll come to his senses. Do you have a late pass, Charlie?

HIGH SCHOOL
LATE PASS
NAME: Charlie Littlemoon
TIME: 8:45
SIGNED: *M. Alvarez*

Charlie: No, sir, I don't. You see, I didn't want to be any later than I had to. So I came right here. I didn't go anywhere near the principal's office.

Darryl: Yet another portentous answer!

Charlie: *(Bewildered)* What is this portentous stuff anyway?

Mr. Nichols: It has to do with a little vocabulary lesson we had before you got here. It seems as if Darryl got somewhat carried away.

Maxine: *(Giggling)* More like he got lost!

Mr. Nichols: Be nice, Maxine. As our resident comic, Darryl keeps things lively for all of us. *(Turning to Charlie Littlemoon)* I'll fill you in later, Charlie. But right now please go get a late pass from Mrs. Álvarez.

Charlie: *(Getting up to leave)* Yes, sir.

Narrator: Charlie walks out of the classroom. Mr. Nichols continues the class.

Mr. Nichols: *(Glancing at his watch again)* Now that we are well into the period without, I might add, having accomplished much, we had best get on with things. That, as we all know, means history.

Sylvia: And history means…

Maxine: Field trips!

Mr. Nichols: It means much more than that, I should hope. But you are right, Maxine. According to our schedule and budget, we can take two more field trips this year. I'd like to suggest a trip to the new wing of the museum.

Susan: Isn't that the part Charlie's grandfather runs?

Mr. Nichols: That's right, Susan. It features the culture of the Plains Indians, including, of course, the Dakota Sioux.

Narrator: Charlie Littlemoon enters the room and puts his late pass on Mr. Nichols's desk.

Sylvia: Isn't that what you are, Charlie—a Dakota Sioux?

Charlie: That's right. My grandfather and I are both Dakota Sioux.

Mr. Nichols: Since we're about to begin a study of Native American cultures, a visit to the museum would be a good way to introduce the unit.

Darryl: Mr. Nichols, can I ask a question?

Mr. Nichols: Go ahead, Darryl.

Darryl: Why do we always study old things? I mean, those old days are gone. What can we learn from them? We need to look ahead, to the future—to space, for example.

Mr. Nichols: If we don't learn about what happened years ago, we might make the same mistakes ourselves. Besides, it's fun to find out how people our own ages lived. Don't you think so?

Darryl: Well, I suppose so. *(Brightening)* Say, you did mention two field trips. I think Charlie should take us on one before we go to the museum.

Mr. Nichols: What do you mean, Darryl?

Darryl: Well, if Charlie showed us how the Sioux used to live—outside, someplace—then the things we'll be reading about and the things we'll see in the museum will be much more real. Don't you think that would make a good field trip?

Susan: That's a great idea, Darryl!

Sylvia: It would be fun, too. We could take a bus out into the country.

Maxine: *(Joining in)* And we'd learn a lot.

Darryl: We would learn much more than we would in school, Mr. Nichols.

Mr. Nichols: Darryl, I'm not so sure about this one. I'm not sure it's a safe trip. Winters can get pretty nasty, even around here. And Charlie might not like the idea.

Charlie: Oh, I wouldn't mind, Mr. Nichols. My grandfather taught me many of the old Sioux ways. He says it's important to learn them. That way, no matter where I live, I will never forget who I am.

Susan: Please, Mr. Nichols? We'll be in the school bus. It's not like anything could go wrong.

Mr. Nichols: Okay, you've convinced me. I'll set things up with Mrs. Álvarez. *(Handing out permission slips)* Each of you will have to get these permission slips signed by your parents. You will each need to bring a sack lunch that day, too. Have the signed slips in by Friday, and we'll make final plans that day.

Act Two

Narrator: The day of the field trip is cold and clear, but the students are dressed warmly. Charlie is dressed in the kind of clothing the Sioux once wore in the winter. He is wearing a buffalo robe over a buckskin shirt and leggings. His feet are stuffed into sturdy moccasins. In his left hand, he carries a pair of wooden snowshoes. In his right, he holds a short bow and a handful of arrows. Thrown over one shoulder is a pouch made of hide. Seeing Charlie, the students immediately begin asking him questions. Mr. Nichols quickly steps in.

Mr. Nichols: Charlie can answer your questions on the bus, kids. Right now we'd better get going, or we'll use up all our time in the parking lot.

Narrator: Filled with chattering students, the bus heads north on Highway 83. Several miles later, driver Rosalie Young turns onto a dirt trail and drives east for an hour. When the trail disappears, she brings the bus to a stop.

Rosalie: How does this spot look, Mr. Nichols?

Mr. Nichols: I think we'd better ask Charlie.

Charlie: This will do fine, Mr. Nichols.

Darryl: Do fine for what? I don't see anything anywhere but brown grass. There are no trees or bushes!

Mr. Nichols: That's exactly right, Darryl. This looks as close to the Great Plains as we can get in our part of the state. *(Turning to Charlie)* Charlie Littlemoon, I give you the eighth grade.

Narrator: For the better part of two hours, Charlie Littlemoon talks about life on the Great Plains as it was a hundred years ago. He retells stories his grandfather has told him about hunting buffalo and schools and the games children played. He talks about Sioux customs and laws and religion. His classmates are so interested that they don't notice the sky has turned a dark gray. In a few minutes, the temperature drops quickly. The wind roars out of the north like a buffalo stampede. Mr. Nichols turns to Rosalie with a worried look on his face.

Mr. Nichols: Is this what I think it is, Rosalie?

Rosalie: Sure looks like the start of a blizzard to me. We better get going.

Mr. Nichols: Right you are. Okay, everyone on the bus. Let's get a move on!

Narrator: As soon as the students are on the bus, Rosalie starts back down the dirt trail toward the highway. But within minutes, visibility is near zero in a blinding snow that is deepening rapidly. Rosalie stops the bus.

Rosalie: That's it, Mr. Nichols. We're not going anywhere. In this weather, I can't tell north from south. We'll wait out the storm right here.

Mr. Nichols: Whatever you think, Rosalie. We've got plenty of food and water and warm clothing. Let's hope the storm blows through as fast as it arrived.

Narrator: But the storm rages on into the night. An uneasy silence settles over the students. Mr. Nichols tries to sound calm.

Mr. Nichols: Okay, gang, the great adventure begins. We'll be here a few hours more, so make yourselves comfortable. Try to sleep. Rosalie and I will take turns staying awake. One of us will start the engine every hour to get some heat in here. Don't worry, though. Help will arrive soon.

Darryl: *(Sounding frightened)* Who do you think is coming, Mr. Nichols? And how will anybody know where we are?

Mr. Nichols: Mrs. Álvarez knows where we are. She'll notify the road department, and road crews will be on their way with snowplows.

Sylvia: She knows we started out on Highway 83, Darryl.

Darryl: *(Groaning)* She doesn't know where we turned off the road! We'll freeze to death before anyone finds us. We're goners, I tell you!

Mr. Nichols: There's nothing to be frightened about, Darryl. Help will be here by morning. I promise.

Darryl: It sure better be.

Susan: Oh, Darryl, don't be such a baby.

Narrator: Mr. Nichols sees that everyone has enough blankets for the night, and then he takes his own seat. No sooner has he settled in than Charlie appears.

Charlie: *(Whispering)* Mr. Nichols, how can you be sure we'll be found soon?

Mr. Nichols: I…well…the truth is, I'm not so sure at all.

Charlie: Let me go for help, Mr. Nichols. I know what to do.

Mr. Nichols: Are you crazy, Charlie? Why, we don't even know where the main road is.

Charlie: But, Mr. Nichols!

Mr. Nichols: It's out of the question, Charlie. Go back to your seat and get some sleep. That's what I'm going to do.

Readers' Theater, SV 6175-3

Act Three

Narrator: With the first light of day, Mr. Nichols wakes with a start.

Mr. Nichols: *(To himself)* I must have dozed off. *(Looking out the window)* Good, the storm passed. The wind is down, too. *(Checking his watch)* It's just a few minutes after seven. I'll let the kids sleep as long as they can.

Narrator: Mr. Nichols walks the aisle, checking on his students. Suddenly he stops.

Mr. Nichols: Charlie! Where's Charlie?

Susan: *(Whispering)* Mr. Nichols, Charlie left the bus just before sunrise.

Mr. Nichols: *(Alarmed)* He what?

Susan: He said he was going for help. He made me promise not to tell you.

Mr. Nichols: Oh, no! Why would he do such a foolish thing? He'll never find the road.

Narrator: Mr. Nichols sinks into his seat, holding his head in his hands.

Susan: Don't worry, Mr. Nichols. Charlie said he knew what he was doing. I believe him.

Mr. Nichols: I hope so, Susan. I sure hope so.

Narrator: Susan curls up in her seat. Mr. Nichols stares blankly out the window.

Darryl: *(Sitting up with a start)* Listen, everyone! An engine. Do you hear it? Wake up, you guys!

Maxine: *(Sleepily)* Huh? What's going on?

Sylvia: Go back to sleep, Maxine. It's only Darryl.

Susan: Quiet, Darryl. You'll wake everyone.

Darryl: But that's what I want to do! Can't you hear it? It's a truck. Listen!

Narrator: Darryl's excited voice wakes the other students. Soon they see a truck armed with a snowplow mounted on the front. Students cheer as the truck grinds to a halt by the school bus. Charlie Littlemoon leaps down from the cab and runs to the bus. He is followed closely by his grandfather and Rob Grant, who is driving the truck.

Charlie: Mr. Nichols! I found the snowplow on the road and led Mr. Grant and my grandfather here! They have been looking for us all night!

Rob: *(Approaching Mr. Nichols)* Is everybody okay, Mr. Nichols?

Mr. Nichols: *(Sounding relieved)* Everyone's fine, thank you. Everyone is just fine.

Darryl: Am I ever glad to see you, Charlie!

Mr. Nichols: *(Turning to Walter Littlemoon)* You must be Charlie's grandfather.

Walter: I am, Mr. Nichols, and I'm extremely proud of my grandson today.

Rob: You sure should be, Walter. Young Charlie here is one smart fellow. How he found the road—let alone us—is beyond me.

Mr. Nichols: How did you do it, Charlie? The snow must be two feet deep, and there's not a single landmark in sight.

Charlie: Finding the road was easy, Mr. Nichols.

Darryl: *(Breaking in)* Yes, how did you find it, Charlie? How did you do it? Come on, tell us!

Charlie: *(Grinning)* I will if you give me a chance, Darryl. *(Continuing)* I used an old Sioux method my grandfather taught me. I knew we had traveled north on Highway 83 and then turned off it to travel east. So I slipped out of the bus before sunrise. When the sun rose, I turned my back to it. Then I knew I was facing west, toward the highway.

Darryl: *(Impatiently)* Then what, Charlie?

Charlie: I shot an arrow straight ahead of me, and I snowshoed to it. I stood in front of that arrow, making sure my back was still to the sun. Then I shot another arrow ahead of me. I kept doing this until I reached the road, which was already plowed.

Darryl: But what good did the arrows do?

Susan: Honestly, Darryl, sometimes I worry about you.

Sylvia: By shooting the arrows, Charlie made sure he was walking in a straight line.

Maxine: Then the truck followed the arrows back to the bus.

Darryl: Oh, now I see.

Walter: That is how the Sioux found their way across the Great Plains before they had compasses.

Darryl: That's great! Charlie, can you teach us some more of those Sioux things?

Charlie: Sure, Darryl, I'll be glad to, once we get back home.

Mr. Nichols: Speaking of which, I think we've had quite enough adventure for one field trip. Let's start back.

Students: *(Together)* Hooray!

Rob: Just follow me, Rosalie. I'll clear a better path for the bus.

Mr. Nichols: By the way, Darryl, do you still think the old days don't have any meaning for us today?

Darryl: Did I say that, Mr. Nichols? If I did, I sure didn't mean it. History's my favorite subject!

Students: *(Groaning)* Oh, Darryl!

MEET THE PLAYERS

Character	Reading Level
Narrator	4.9
Josefina (ho say FEE nah) "Joey" Guerrero, *a spy for the Filipino underground*	4.8
Renato (ray NAH to) Guerrero, *Joey's husband*	4.2
Dr. Garza, *a medical doctor*	6.6
Carmen Díaz, *Joey's neighbor*	4.5
Servero Díaz, *Carmen's husband*	2.4
Manuel Colayco (ko LY ko), *a leader of the Filipino underground*	5.6
Japanese Soldier	2.0
Japanese Officer	2.0
American Soldier	2.0

PLAY SUMMARY

In late 1941, Joey Guerrero learns she has contracted Hansen's Disease — leprosy. Because of this, she must send her daughter away for several years while she recovers from the disease. Then the Japanese attack Pearl Harbor and the Philippine Islands. Joey is asked to work with the Filipino underground. She risks her life to report on the activities of the Japanese occupation forces and to carry an invaluable map to the American forces who are fighting to free the Philippines. After the war, a grateful American government gives Joey a medal and sends her to a hospital in the United States, where she is cured of leprosy.

Note: This play is based on a true story.

VOCABULARY

While the character parts of *Joey's Private War* are written to accommodate a variety of reading levels, you may wish to use the following words in vocabulary activities.

drawn tight, p. 53
condemn, p. 54
leper, pp. 54, 64, 67
strides, p. 54
take heart, p. 55
underground,
pp. 58, 60, 63, 64,
65, 68
movement, p. 58

breaks, p. 59
detail, p. 60
closely, p. 61
timidly, p. 61
mangoes, p. 62
papayas, p. 62
despite, p. 62
cause, pp. 62, 64

invaluable, p. 62
jeering, p. 62
scrawl, p. 65
minefields, pp. 65, 68
mission, p. 66
traces, p. 69

TAPPING PRIOR KNOWLEDGE

Before reading *Joey's Private War*, you may wish to discuss the following questions with students.

1. Years ago a disease called leprosy struck many people. Other people thought they could catch the disease by touching or being near lepers. As a result, the sick were forced to live in isolation. Do you think people who have serious illnesses should be treated this way? Explain your answer.

2. Suppose you were asked to do something that meant risking your life in order to help your country defeat an enemy. Would you agree to do it? Why or why not?

3. How would you feel if you got sick and were told you could not see your family until you got better, no matter how long that took?

4. Suppose your town was invaded by soldiers from another country, who took away your rights and forced you to obey them without question. Which right would you miss the most? How would you feel about your captors? Would you try to do something to change your situation? If so, what would you do?

5. Think of a hero who risked his or her life for a cause. What did that person do to earn the title "hero"? What traits make this person someone to be admired?

THINKING IT OVER

The following questions may be used in a variety of ways after students read *Joey's Private War*. Each question may be discussed orally as a class or in small groups, or it may be answered as part of a written classroom or homework assignment.

1. After Joey found out she had leprosy, what was she afraid she wouldn't have the strength to do?

2. From the beginning of the occupation, how did Joey react to the way the Japanese soldiers were treating the Filipinos?

3. Why were Servero and Carmen taking a chance when they told Joey about their underground activities?

4. Why was Joey sent to walk the waterfront for the Filipino underground?

5. What is one example from the play that shows how dangerous Joey's work for the underground was?

6. Why did Renato protest when Joey was asked to take messages from the leader of the underground to the freedom fighters in the hills?

7. What reason did Manuel Colayco give for wanting Joey to be his messenger? How did Joey's husband react? How did Joey react?

8. How did Joey's leprosy help her pass safely through the Japanese lines on her way to the American lines?

PRESENTING THE PLAY

Radio Play

The following sound effects will help you present *Joey's Private War* as a radio play.

- taped music to indicate act breaks — pp. 53, 56, 57, 60, 62, 65, 67
- battle sounds, including bombs — Act Two, p. 57; Act Seven, p. 65; Act Eight, p. 67
- knocking on a door — Act Three, p. 57
- clock ticking — Act Three, p. 59
- people and traffic at the waterfront — Act Four, pp. 61–62
- airplanes roaring overhead — Act Seven, p. 65

Classroom Play

All the sound effects listed for the radio play can also be used to stage the play in the classroom. Additionally, you may wish to use the props listed below.

- desk and chairs for doctor's office — Act One, pp. 53–55
- bench — Act One, pp. 55–56
- table to use as a bed, blanket, and pillow — Act Two, p. 56; Act Eight, p. 68
- chairs arranged as sofa — Act Three, p. 58; Act Five, p. 62
- basket filled with fruit — Act Four, pp. 61–62
- paper for a letter — Act Seven, pp. 65–66
- map — Act Seven, pp. 65–66; Act Eight, p. 68

EXTENDING THE PLAY

You may wish to use some of the following activities to enrich the students' reading of *Joey's Private War.*

1. The blackline masters included in this Teacher's Guide can be duplicated for use with any of the *Readers' Theater* plays.
2. Have students research the disease leprosy and report their findings to the class.
3. Have students imagine that they are Joey about to receive a medal from the Americans. Tell them to write an acceptance speech and present it to the class.
4. Have students research the lives of other notable spies during World War II. Then have them write a short biographical sketch about a spy.
5. Have students design posters to convince people to enlist in the Filipino underground movement.
6. Have students write a poem in honor of Joey Guerrero's heroic deeds.
7. Have students make up a code that freedom fighters in the underground movement might use to send messages to one another.

Joey's Private War

by Laurence Swinburne

Cast
(in order of appearance)

Narrator

Renato Guerrero, *Joey's husband*

Josefina "Joey" Guerrero, *a spy for the Filipino underground*

Dr. Garza, *a medical doctor*

Carmen Díaz, *Joey's neighbor*

Servero Díaz, *Carmen's husband*

Japanese Soldier

Manuel Colayco, *a leader of the Filipino underground*

Japanese Officer

American Soldier

52   Readers' Theater, SV 6175-3

Act One

Narrator: It is late autumn in 1941. A young woman and her husband sit in a doctor's waiting room. The woman's face is drawn tight. She keeps wringing her hands nervously. From time to time, her husband pats her arm. He tries to put on as brave a face as he can.

Renato: I'm sure everything will be fine.

Joey: Oh, how I want to believe you, Renato. But even if you are a doctor, you can't tell if these swellings on my arms and legs are nothing to be worried about.

Renato: Perhaps I can't, Joey. But Dr. Garza will know. He's an expert.

Narrator: The door to an inner office opens. A grave-looking Dr. Garza calls Renato and Joey inside.

Dr. Garza: Please sit down. *(Pauses)* I am sorry to have kept you waiting so long. I had to be certain of the test results. *(Another pause)* Mrs. Guerrero, I have made this announcement many times, but I have never found a way to say it without causing pain. So I will simply say—Mrs. Guerrero, you have leprosy.

Joey: *(Gasping)* Leprosy!

Renato: No, it can't be!

Dr. Garza: That is the bad news. But don't lose hope.

Joey: *(Bitterly)* Hope? You condemn me to a life of a leper! I may see myself changed into a person that people hide from in fear! Don't you know the law here in the Philippines, Dr. Garza? Lepers must ring a bell wherever they go. That is so the "clean" people can get out of their way! You speak to me of hope? It's better to be dead!

Renato: Please listen to Dr. Garza, Joey. He says there's hope. It must be so.

Dr. Garza: There have been great strides made in the search for a cure for leprosy, or Hansen's disease, as we doctors prefer to call it. Rest will help. And now we have medicines, too.

Renato: How long will this treatment take, Dr. Garza?

Dr. Garza: I think it can take two, three, maybe four years. Joey must follow my directions carefully. There's one more thing that I must tell you.

Joey: And what is that?

Dr. Garza: I understand you have a child—an infant girl.

Joey: We do. Cynthia is just two years old.

Dr. Garza: She must be sent away—until you're cured.

Joey: *(Horrified)* Sent away? Never!

Dr. Garza: You must do this! You must never kiss or even touch her until you are completely cured. You see, while there is little chance any adult will get Hansen's disease from you, the same is not true of children. We don't know why. *(Brightens)* But take heart, Mrs. Guerrero. With rest and the proper medicine, you'll conquer this disease! Then you'll have lots of time to spend with your family.

Narrator: Joey and Renato leave Dr. Garza's office. They are very saddened by the news. Outside they find a bench in a quiet corner of a small park. There they sit, deep in thought.

Joey: The sickness—the leprosy—I can take, Renato. I may be only 5 feet tall and weigh just 100 pounds, but I'm strong. I've been sick before, and each time I got well. And I'm only 23 years old. But to give up Cynthia—I'm not sure I have that kind of strength.

Renato: *(Softly)* It is hard. But you must, Josefina. You must do it. Cynthia must be kept safe!

Joey: *(Smiling through her tears)* Josefina? You haven't called me by that name since the first time we met, Renato.

Renato: Then let this be a new first, Josefina. Together we'll lick this disease!

Act Two

Narrator: Within three weeks, more trouble awaits Joey and Renato. This news is bad for all the people of the Philippines.

Renato: Joey, wake up! Wake up! I have very bad news!

Joey: *(Sleepily)* Renato, is that you? But it's still dark. Why aren't you at the hospital? What time is it? *(Now fully awake)* Renato, why are your hands shaking so? Your face is so pale!

Renato: It's nearly morning. But never mind the time. Joey, the Japanese have attacked Pearl Harbor. That is the American naval base in Hawaii. Soon the Japanese will be bombing us. Their army will follow. We're at war!

Joey: What will we do?

Renato: All we can do is pray and hope. I don't know what else to do.

Narrator: Before long, a battle takes place throughout the Philippine Islands. American soldiers fight side by side with the Filipino army. But their numbers are small. Soon they are forced to give up.

Joey: We have lost our islands, Renato. We must run into the hills to continue the fight.

Renato: We can't, Joey. You need your medicine and your rest. Both will be hard enough to get here. They will be impossible to get in the hills. And I have my work, too. There are the wounded and the sick. I must stay and help them.

Joey: If only there were something I could do.

Act Three

Narrator: Late one afternoon there is a knock on the Guerrero's door. Joey opens it and sees a small woman.

Carmen: *(In a whisper)* My name is Carmen Díaz, Mrs. Guerrero. My husband and I live upstairs in apartment 33. Please come see us tonight at eight o'clock. We have something important to talk over with you.

Joey: What is this all about?

Carmen: *(Whispering)* Tonight—at eight—and you will learn all.

Narrator: Joey wonders what the woman wants. Renato is working the night shift at the hospital. At eight o'clock she goes to apartment 33.

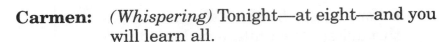

Carmen: Mrs. Guerrero, come in, quickly! We're never sure who may be watching.

Narrator: A man who is seated on a sofa stands and holds out his hand.

Servero: I am Servero Díaz, Mrs. Guerrero. I heard how you stand up to the Japanese soldiers, not letting them bully you.

Joey: I'm angry. They have no right to stop and search anyone.

Servero: You seem like a woman of courage, Mrs. Guerrero. So much so that Carmen and I are going to put our lives in your hands.

Joey: Your lives? But how? Why?

Carmen: We are part of the underground movement. The Japanese call us spies. But we are freedom fighters. We want only to win back our country. That's why we're building a new army. This army will fight by gathering information for the time the Americans return.

Servero: Mrs. Guerrero, you have three choices. You can betray us to the Japanese. You can forget about this meeting and get on with your life. Or you can join us.

Narrator: The sound of a clock ticking is all that is heard for several minutes. Then...

Joey: You must know I would never turn in a Filipino to the Japanese. Your secret is safe with me. Since I...*(Her voice breaks.)* no longer have a daughter to care for, and my husband works long hours at the hospital, I will join you. What will you have me do?

Carmen: For now we want you to watch the soldiers who live across the street. We want to know all about them. Do they seem strong or tired? How do they live? What foods do they eat?

Servero: And how many trucks come and go in a day? Where do they go? What do they bring? Then...

Joey: *(Interrupting)* I don't mind. But why don't you two do that? After all, what I can see from my apartment is no more than you can see from here. Besides, what you want doesn't sound very important.

Carmen: Perhaps not to you, Mrs. Guerrero. But think of all this as the parts of a recipe. The things you tell us will be added to facts we get from others. Put all together, and they become important indeed.

Servero: My wife and I own a shoe store across the city. It's near the Japanese army headquarters. That's the building we watch.

Act Four

Narrator: So Joey becomes a spy for the Filipino underground. At first the work she does is easy. She stands behind thick curtains in her apartment. Joey writes down the things she sees go on in the building across the street.

Servero: In a week you've given us more information than we could have gotten in a year, Joey. You have a good eye for detail.

Carmen: Now we have a tougher job for you. We want you to walk the waterfront. The Japanese have hidden many big guns there. We must learn where they are. Then the American planes can destroy them.

Narrator: This is a risky job. Japanese guards watch all Filipinos closely. But Joey finds a fruit store nearby. She visits it often, trying to look like all the other shoppers. No one looks at her until one day…

Japanese Soldier: Hey, you there. *(Pointing at Joey)* Yes, you, girl.

Joey: *(In a frightened voice)* Me, sir?

Japanese Soldier: What's that in your basket?

Joey: *(Timidly)* Only fresh fruit for my sick husband, sir.

Japanese Soldier: What does he matter when a soldier of the emperor is hungry for fresh fruit. Give me the basket!

Narrator: Joey's heart nearly stops when the soldier takes the basket from her hands. On top of the fruit pile is a hollow pineapple. This is where Joey hides her notes. The soldier picks up the pineapple.

Japanese Soldier: This one looks juicy enough.

Narrator: He goes to stuff the pineapple into his pack. Then he stops.

Japanese Soldier: No, wait. I've had pineapples every day for a week. I've had enough of them!

Joey: There are mangoes in the basket, sir—and papayas, too. Perhaps you'd like them better?

Japanese Soldier: So I would, girl; so I would.

Narrator: The soldier empties the basket of mangoes and papayas. Then he shoves it at Joey, who takes it with trembling hands.

Japanese Soldier: *(Jeering)* I see you are afraid, girl. That is wise, for the emperor's soldiers are like giants among the Filipinos. Here, take the pineapples to your sick man. May he choke on them!

Act Five

Narrator: Despite that close brush with death, Joey takes on more dangerous jobs. She is very good at each one. Even Renato joins in the cause. Then one evening Joey and Renato are called to the Díaz's apartment. A man in his forties greets them. He has serious, brown eyes.

Carmen: Joey and Renato, may I present Captain Manuel Colayco.

Manuel: I'm honored to meet you both. *(To Renato)* Doctor, the information you have picked up in the hospital has been invaluable. *(To Joey)* And you, Mrs. Guerrero, your work has been magnificent. All Filipinos will honor you someday.

Joey: Sir, to have the leader of the Filipino underground in the city address me this way is embarrassing. I'm just a small worker among many.

Manuel: Small in size, perhaps, but great in importance. Each day brings us closer to the American invasion—thanks greatly to the work of people such as you.

Carmen: Do you think the invasion will come soon, Manuel?

Manuel: *(Smiling)* Sooner than you think. But there's still much work to be done.

Renato: We're ready.

Manuel: You will need to be, Dr. Guerrero. Once the invasion begins, there will be great need of your services at the hospital.

Joey: And will there be work for me?

Manuel: Mrs. Guerrero, you're the main reason why I'm here. We need someone to work between my headquarters here in the city and the underground fighters in the hills. I can't rely on radios to do the job. I need your help.

Renato: This is foolish, Captain Colayco. My wife is too weak and too sick for this. Why, even now she's done too much. She…

Manuel: I know about her sickness, Dr. Guerrero. And she's free to refuse, of course. But let me add it is because your wife is a leper that we…

Renato: *(Angrily)* Do not use the word *leper*. Josefina has Hansen's disease.

Manuel: *(Calmly)* That's a better term by far, I agree. And what do you think will be the reaction of enemy soldiers when they see her? I know we're using her illness to further our own cause. But after all, it's the Republic of the Philippines we're trying to save!

Joey: It's all right, Renato. Don't worry, Captain Colayco. I'll be your messenger.

Narrator: Joey Guerrero knows what Captain Colayco means about her health. In the past few months, she has gotten much worse. She has not been able to get any medicine. Her spying keeps her from getting the rest she needs. She looks painfully different. Still, she goes on her first trip the next night. And night after night beyond that, she takes the dangerous route through Japanese lines out of the city and into the hills where the underground fighters await her. Her work is of great value to Captain Colayco. It is also very hard on Joey's health.

Act Six

Narrator: A few weeks later, Captain Colayco speaks to Joey about her health.

Manuel: Mrs. Guerrero, I think you've done enough. Frankly, you are very ill.

Joey: *(Determined)* I won't stop until the last Japanese soldier has been driven from our country.

Manuel: You have a wonderful spirit, Mrs. Guerrero. But I insist you must rest. There will be more work for you later. For now, go into the hills to rest at the underground camp there.

Act Seven

Narrator: Joey's rest period does not last long. Day after day American planes roar overhead. Many of them attack the guns Joey has found for them. Then on October 20, 1944, the Americans land from the sea. The invasion begins. Soon the Americans are nearing Manila, the capital city, from the north. Captain Colayco writes Joey a letter.

Manuel: *(Reading)* Dear Mrs. Guerrero: Please excuse my scrawl, but I'm writing in a big hurry. I've enclosed a map of the country north of Manila. It shows the safe routes through the Japanese minefields. It is most important the Americans get this map as soon as possible. The Japanese are everywhere along the route the Americans must take. I believe you are the one person who might—I say "might," since I won't pretend this mission is not dangerous—get through. Good luck. Our country owes you much for what you have already done.

Narrator: Joey has the map taped to her back. Then she starts for the American lines. She is sick with a fever and a headache. Her feet are so swollen she cannot wear shoes. And the sores on her body—especially on her face—have gotten worse. Still, she goes on, trying to reach the American lines in the daylight. She is well on her way when she is stopped.

Japanese Officer: You there! What are you doing here?

Joey: *(Weakly)* What does war mean to me? I'm sick and wish to go home to die.

Narrator: Joey waves her hand toward the north, as if pointing in the direction of her home.

Japanese Officer: Well, you can't go that way. There's heavy fighting up there. Come over here so I can get a closer look at you.

Narrator: Joey walks toward the Japanese officer. She worries that he'll have her searched. Then the officer sees her face close up. He gasps and steps back.

Japanese Officer: You are a leper! Get away from me, woman!

Joey: Will you let me go home, sir?

Japanese Officer: Yes, yes, go! You won't make it, but it is your choice. Now get out of here!

Narrator: As Joey moves on, she hears the Japanese officer say to a soldier nearby...

Japanese Officer: I almost feel sorry for her. She'll not live long, even if she does make it home. She may be better off if she's killed on the way.

Act Eight

Narrator: Joey Guerrero does not die. Although shells drop near her at times, she makes it to the American lines.

American Soldier: Hold your fire! There's a woman approaching. *(To Joey)* Hey, lady, what are you doing out there? Don't you realize that what you're doing is very dangerous? Are you nuts or something? *(Then he sees her face.)* What happened to you? Let me take you to a doctor.

Joey: There's no time for that! I have a map of the minefields the underground gave me. I must take it to your commanding officer!

Narrator: She does deliver the map. Thanks to the map, American soldiers are able to move into Manila quickly, saving the lives of many. There is great joy in the city, but there is sadness, too.

Joey: Renato, I'm so glad to see you again. I thought for a time…

Renato: Hush, Joey. You're safe. Now you must rest. You can't go on.

Joey: I will, Renato. You can't know how much pain I have or how very tired I am. But I have one more duty to perform. I must report to Captain Colayco.

Renato: As a doctor, I should say no. As your husband, I'll say yes. It's only because I know you've made up your mind to do this. Joey, Captain Colayco is in the hospital. Let's go there.

Narrator: Captain Colayco lies in a hospital bed, barely able to breathe. He has been badly hurt in the battle for Manila.

Joey: *(In tears)* Captain Colayco, I have delivered your map.

Manuel: *(In a tired, weak voice)* You did well, Mrs. Guerrero. You're a true hero.

Narrator: Within hours, Manuel Colayco dies from his wounds. But that is not the end of Joey Guerrero's story.

When the war ends, she is flown to the United States. She is awarded the Medal of Freedom with Silver Palm, the highest honor for war service by a civilian. Then she is transported to a hospital where she receives special treatment for her disease. Long rest and newly developed medicines do their job. At last the final traces of leprosy disappear, and Joey Guerrero is able to lead a normal life again. Josefina "Joey" Guerrero's private war is over. She has won.

MEET THE PLAYERS

Character	Reading Level
Narrator	6.2
Marcos Pérez, *a scientist*	5.4
Adela Pérez, *a scientist*	5.7
Sergeant Walter O'Hara, *a police officer*	2.7
Annie Mercer, *an assistant to the mayor*	3.5
Pamela Lee, *a newspaper editor*	2.9
Lieutenant Henry Thompson, *a police officer*	5.0
Officer Stan Metcalf, *a police officer*	2.4
Officer Sarah Michaud, *a police officer*	2.1
Radio Voice	5.8

PLAY SUMMARY

Marcos and Adela Pérez are scientists trying to discover evidence of life on other planets by picking up radio signals from outer space. One day they hear a voice on their radio that seems to be predicting events one day in advance. The voice predicts sports scores and that a local bridge will collapse, causing the death of one person. Marcos and Adela are rebuffed when they try to warn the police, the mayor, and the newspaper about the bridge. Then they go back to the police and try using the next day's football scores as "proof" of their claim. When the police learn the scores are correct, they rush to close the bridge. Marcos rescues a young girl, but he is unable to save himself.

VOCABULARY

While the character parts of *The Tomorrow Radio* are written to accommodate a variety of reading levels, you may wish to use the following words in vocabulary activities.

project, p. 75
eventful, p. 75
breakthrough, p. 76
opening-round, p. 76
sound waves, p. 77
upset, pp. 77, 86
update, p. 78
stay tuned, pp. 79, 91

details, pp. 79, 84, 91
evidence, p. 81
convenient, p. 84
obviously, p. 84
frustrated, p. 85
admit, p. 86
according to, p. 86

antics, p. 87
pounding a beat, p. 87
coincidence, p. 88
girders, pp. 89, 90
hesitantly, p. 90
intently, p. 90

TAPPING PRIOR KNOWLEDGE

Before reading *The Tomorrow Radio*, you may wish to discuss the following questions with students.

1. Do you think it is more important for scientists to learn whether there is life on other planets or to try to solve problems we have on Earth? Explain your answer.

2. Would you like to know what will happen tomorrow? What advantages can you think of for knowing tomorrow's events? What are the disadvantages? What specific things would you want to know? What would you do with the information once you had it? What would you not want to know?

3. If you had the chance to save someone's life at the risk of losing your own, would you do so? Explain your answer.

THINKING IT OVER

The following questions may be used in a variety of ways after students read *The Tomorrow Radio*. Each question may be discussed orally as a class or in small groups, or it may be answered as part of a written classroom or homework assignment.

1. What information were Adela and Marcos trying to get from their radio? Why were they surprised by the broadcast?

2. The radio voice spoke as if that day were Saturday, but Adela and Marcos knew it was Friday. How did they know that they had not just lost track of time while working in the lab?

3. Why did Adela write down the football scores?

4. What did Marcos mean when he said that the radio could start a war if it got into the wrong hands?

5. Why was Adela hesitant to go to the police with the information about the bridge collapsing?

6. Why did Sergeant Walter O'Hara think Adela and Marcos might need to be locked up?

7. Why was everyone reluctant to believe Marcos and Adela at first?

8. What did the administrative assistant to the mayor tell Adela and Marcos to do when they told her about the bridge collapsing?

9. Why did Lieutenant Thompson finally order Sergeant O'Hara to close the bridge?

10. If Adela and Marcos had not heard the broadcast, would the results of the bridge disaster have been the same? Explain your answer.

PRESENTING THE PLAY

Radio Play

The following sound effects will help you present *The Tomorrow Radio* as a radio play.

- taped music to indicate act breaks — pp. 75, 82, 84, 85, 86, 88
- radio static — Act One, pp. 76–79;
- radio music — Act One, p. 78; Act Six, p. 91
- car engine running — Act Two, p. 82
- sound of traffic and people leaving bridge — Act Six, p. 89
- woman screaming — Act Six, p. 90
- running footsteps — Act Six, p. 91
- noises of bridge collapsing — Act Six, p. 91
- people screaming — Act Six, p. 91

Classroom Play

All the sound effects listed for the radio play can also be used to stage the play in the classroom. Additionally, you may wish to use the props listed below.

- table for radio — Act One, pp. 75–81
- the experimental radio — Act One, pp. 75–81
- newspaper — Act One, p. 78
- pencil and paper — Act One, pp. 78, 81; Act Three, p. 85; Act Five, pp. 86–87
- desks and chairs for police station — Act Two, pp. 82–83; Act Four, pp. 85–86
- desktop radio — Act Five, p. 87
- car radio — Act Six, p. 91

EXTENDING THE PLAY

You may wish to use some of the following activities to enrich the students' reading of *The Tomorrow Radio*.

1. The blackline masters included in this Teacher's Guide can be duplicated for use with any of the *Readers' Theater* plays.

2. Have students write alternative titles for the play.

3. Have students write a folk song entitled "The Ballad of Marcos Pérez," which retells the story of his heroic deed.

4. Have students design the front page of a newspaper to tell about the collapse of River Bridge. Tell them to include illustrations, headlines, interviews, and general news stories in the front-page newspaper layout.

5. Have students write one or two paragraphs about what they would do if they knew a bridge in their town was going to collapse tomorrow.

6. Have students design a plaque to be put on Somerville's new bridge as a memorial to Marcos Pérez.

The Tomorrow Radio

by Robyn Reeves

Cast
(in order of appearance)

Narrator

Marcos Pérez, *a scientist*

Adela Pérez, *a scientist*

Radio Voice

Sergeant Walter O'Hara, *a police officer*

Annie Mercer, *an assistant to the mayor*

Pamela Lee, *a newspaper editor*

Lieutenant Henry Thompson

Officer Stan Metcalf } *police officers*

Officer Sarah Michaud

Act One

Narrator: Marcos and Adela Pérez, a husband-and-wife team of scientists, are working on a project in their lab at home. For several years they have been trying to discover evidence of life on other planets by picking up radio signals from deep in outer space. Their work has been expensive, however, and their money is about to run out. But on this eventful Friday afternoon, a much greater crisis awaits them.

Marcos: Why don't we close up for the night, Adela? I'm beat. Anyway, it's almost five o'clock.

Adela: Okay, Marcos, I'm pretty tired myself. *(Pauses)* This stupid radio. You'd think that because of all the time and money we have put into it, we'd come up with something more than static and an occasional clicking noise.

Marcos: We'll come up with something. I'm sure of it.

Adela: We may never have the chance if we don't get some money fast. We can barely afford the bill for electricity in the lab. We've got to have more money.

Marcos: All we can do is keep on working. We'll have a breakthrough sooner or later. We just have to hang in there somehow until it happens.

Adela: I guess we don't have much choice. *(Pauses)* Marcos, give me just five minutes more with this radio, okay? I want to see if I can clear up the static any.

Narrator: Adela turns back to the radio and works with the controls. The static changes its pitch, and a new sound can faintly be heard.

Adela: Marcos, wait a minute.

Marcos: What is it?

Adela: I'm not sure. It sounds like—words.

Narrator: The sounds become clearer, and Marcos and Adela are able to make out a voice.

Radio Voice: Jennifer Capriati and Michael Chang won their opening matches at the tennis tournament today. That will add still more drama to the remaining opening-round play later this evening. And now, a weather forecast for Sunday.

Adela: What next? I never thought we'd be crossing sound waves with an ordinary radio broadcast. Unless there's a Jennifer Capriati who plays tennis on Venus.

Radio Voice: Today's rain will turn into light showers tonight. Tonight will be slightly cooler. Sunday will be mostly cloudy. The high will be in the low fifties. There is a slight chance for clear skies late in the afternoon. The time now is 4:50 P.M.

Adela: That's odd. It's not raining here. The announcer said "tomorrow's weather" and then talked about the weather for Sunday. But tomorrow is Saturday.

Marcos: Know what else is strange? I thought the tennis tournament wasn't supposed to start until Saturday. But the announcer said the opening matches were already over.

Adela: Maybe this is some kind of joke.

Radio Voice: Here are today's football scores. Dartmouth beat Yale in New Haven, 20 to 17. And here's a big upset. Indiana stunned Ohio State, 35 to 7! In the South…*(Static)*

Adela: This is incredible! How could he have the football scores now? None of these games will be played until tomorrow.

Readers' Theater, SV 6175-3

Or else, Marcos, could we possibly have missed an entire day, working here in the lab?

Marcos: Are you kidding? I have today's paper right here. It says Friday, November 6. It's Friday all right.

Adela: Then I don't get it. This is no ordinary broadcast. It sounds like this radio is somehow a day ahead of us.

Narrator: Marcos and Adela stare at one another, as if searching for answers to their questions. Then Adela reaches for a pencil and begins to write quickly.

Marcos: *(Looking over her shoulder)* What are you doing?

Adela: I'm writing down the football scores. If this thing is as good as it seems to be, we may never have to worry about money again!

Radio Voice: And that's the last of the football scores. This completes our broadcast day. Join me tomorrow, Sunday, at 10:00 A.M. for a sports and weather update. Until then…*(Music plays, then static)*

Marcos: I still can't believe it. A radio that tells the future! Einstein himself would have fainted over this discovery!

Adela: We'll be rich, Marcos! If we bet on all these teams, we can get enough money to support our work for years!

Marcos: But there's more to it than that, Adela. Think of all the good people could do if they knew what was going to happen a day early.

Adela: Let's see. If we borrowed money from all our friends and placed bets on all those games…

Marcos: And think of all the bad that could be done, too. If this radio ever got into the wrong hands, it could start a war! Can you imagine?

Narrator: The radio suddenly crackles to life once more.

Radio Voice: I've just been handed a special news bulletin. River Bridge in Somerville has just collapsed. So far, one person is known dead. Stay tuned for more details. *(Static again, then silence)*

Marcos: Did the announcer say River Bridge? Adela, that's just a few miles from here!

Adela: *(Examining the radio)* The radio has gone dead. I'm afraid something may have burned out.

Marcos: Adela, this is important! We can't keep this news about the bridge to ourselves. I think we better go to the police.

Adela: That's fine, Marcos. What are we going to say? That we can predict the future?

Marcos: We can tell them anything, just so long as that bridge is cleared by tomorrow at five o'clock!

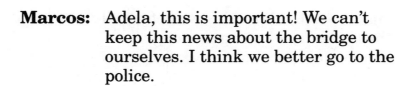

Adela: Okay, Marcos. Any suggestions?

Marcos: Let's just tell them about the radio. We can explain what happened and describe our work.

Adela: I'm sure they'll believe every word. Let's face it, they'll think we're a couple of UFO freaks who have gone off the deep end.

Marcos: We can show them the radio. Then they'll have to believe us.

Adela: Good luck. That radio is dead. And if we can fix it, who knows if it will still give us tomorrow's news?

Marcos: Are you saying we should just forget about this even if we might be able to save someone's life? Don't forget, the announcer said one person was known to be dead.

Adela: I'm not sure. But think about it for a minute. Do you honestly believe we can change the future? We may not be able to stop anything even if we do know about it.

Marcos: But we've got to try!

Adela: What happens if we lose the radio? Suppose the police keep it for evidence?

Marcos: Then I guess we'll have to say good-by to our research money.

Adela: You say that so easily.

Marcos: Adela, you know I'm as desperate as you are to find a way to continue our work. I'd do almost anything to get the money. The thought of having to close the lab is unbearable.

Adela: It's not like we would use the money for something bad. The research we're doing could benefit everybody.

Marcos: I'll leave it up to you, Adela. What do you think we should do?

Narrator: There is a long silence. Then Adela folds up the paper she has written the football scores on and puts it into her pocket.

Adela: Come on, Marcos. We don't have much time. That bridge is going to collapse in less than 24 hours!

Act Two

Narrator: Marcos and Adela drive straight to the local police station. It doesn't take them long to find out what people think of their discovery. In fact, they get no further than Sergeant Walter O'Hara, the officer at the main desk.

Sergeant O'Hara: The River Bridge is going to collapse tomorrow at five o'clock? And just how did you come to find that out?

Marcos: It's kind of hard to explain, Sergeant.

Sergeant O'Hara: I'll just bet it is. You'd better have a good story. I've half a mind to lock you up for making a bomb threat.

Adela: This has nothing to do with bombs, Sergeant. We're scientists, and we've invented a radio that broadcasts 24 hours in advance.

Sergeant O'Hara: A radio that tells the future? Yes, well, I have this aunt who's pretty good with tea leaves. Maybe you should go see her and stop wasting my time.

Marcos: Sergeant, please. You've got to believe us! We're not crazy!

Sergeant O'Hara: Now listen, you two. I've seen some nuts in my time, but you two take the cake. Get out of here, or I'll see that you spend the weekend in the lockup!

Narrator: Discouraged, but not defeated, Marcos and Adela walk to their car.

Marcos: Someone has to listen to us. Maybe the police were the wrong people to go to for help.

Adela: Why not try the mayor?

Marcos: It can't hurt.

Narrator: Soon Marcos and Adela are standing before Annie Mercer, assistant to the mayor of Somerville.

Adela: We'd like to see Mayor Ward, please. It's an emergency.

Annie: I'm sorry, but the mayor is very busy right now. Perhaps you can tell me what the trouble is.

Marcos: River Bridge is going to collapse, and someone will be killed if we don't do something about it!

Annie: May I ask how you found out about this astonishing news?

Marcos: You may find this hard to believe, but we have a radio in our laboratory that broadcasts 24 hours in advance. We heard a news bulletin that the bridge collapsed at five o'clock—tomorrow afternoon. You've got to believe us.

Annie: If you have a radio that broadcasts the future, why haven't you shown it to anyone? That should be enough proof—if what you're saying is really true.

Adela: The radio went dead right after the bulletin.

Annie: Convenient, isn't it? Look, if you are really upset about this, perhaps you'd like to write us a letter describing the details. I can assure you that Mayor Ward reads all his mail.

Act Three

Narrator: Obviously, there isn't time for Marcos and Adela to write a letter. But there is time to try the local newspaper, the *Somerville Tribune*. There they talk to city editor Pamela Lee.

Pamela: I'm sorry, Mr. and Mrs. Pérez. This story is too hard to believe. Why, if I print that and River Bridge doesn't go down, I'll lose my job.

Marcos: But how can we warn everybody? The police, the mayor—no one wants to listen. At five o'clock tomorrow afternoon, that bridge is sure to be filled with traffic.

Adela: And we know at least one person will die. You've got to help!

Pamela: I'm sorry, but I can't afford to take such a chance. Now, if you will excuse me, it's getting late, and I have a paper to put out.

Narrator: Marcos and Adela are frustrated and tired. They walk slowly out of Pamela Lee's office. Suddenly, Adela's face lights up.

Adela: That's it. That's the answer!

Marcos: What's the answer?

Adela: The notes I took of the broadcast! *(She digs them out of her pocket.)* If we take these to the police, they'll find out that we're not crazy after all.

Act Four

Narrator: Sergeant O'Hara is not too happy to see Marcos and Adela again. This time he sends them to Lieutenant Henry Thompson, the watch commander.

Thompson: So, these are the scores of tomorrow's football games?

Adela: Yes, Lieutenant, I promise they are. We didn't make these up. That's the most important list you'll ever look at, believe me!

Dartmouth 20,   Yale 17
Indiana 35,   Ohio State 7
Michigan State 24,   Michigan 17
UCLA 26,   Southern Cal. 24
Oregon State 20,   Oregon 10

Thompson: Now, let's not get too excited, Mrs. Pérez. You have to admit we don't get this kind of news every day.

Marcos: According to the broadcast, the bridge will collapse about 5:00 P.M. tomorrow. The football scores should be in before then. If the scores on this list are right, you'll have time to close the bridge and make sure nobody gets hurt.

Adela: Please, Lieutenant, just copy the scores and hold onto them until tomorrow afternoon. It can't do any harm, can it?

Thompson: Well, I guess not. If by some miracle these scores are right, I guarantee you I'll close the bridge. (*Pauses*) But believe me, if this is your idea of a joke, you'll be hearing from me.

Act Five

Narrator: Late Saturday afternoon Lieutenant Thompson sits at his desk. Officer Stan Metcalf sticks his head through the doorway.

Officer Metcalf: Lieutenant, did you hear about the big upset? Indiana beat Ohio State!

Thompson: (*Suddenly remembering the paper he wrote the scores on*) What time is it, Metcalf?

Officer Metcalf: It's about 4:25. Why?

Narrator: Lieutenant Thompson takes a wrinkled piece of paper from his desk drawer.

Thompson: What was the score, Metcalf?

Officer Metcalf: I think it was 35 to 7.

Thompson: Oh, no! It can't be!

Officer Metcalf: Don't take it so hard, Lieutenant. It's only a game. *(Shouts down the hall)* Hey, everyone, looks like the lieutenant lost a bundle on the Indiana and Ohio State game!

Thompson: Metcalf, antics like that will keep you pounding a beat if you stay 40 years on the police force!

Officer Metcalf: Oh, come on, Lieutenant, I was only kidding. What's so serious about a football game anyway?

Thompson: I'm afraid you're about to find out just how serious this game was, Metcalf!

Narrator: Lieutenant Thompson turns on his desktop radio. He changes stations until he finds a news broadcast. When he does, he is amazed and horrified to learn that every single score on the list is correct.

Thompson: Metcalf, tell Sergeant O'Hara to get two cars over to River Bridge on the double! Have them seal off both entries and clear the bridge. And get Rescue One over there, too. I'm on the way myself. River Bridge is about to collapse!

Act Six

Narrator: Lieutenant Thompson dashes out of the station. Within minutes, he is at the bridge. There he finds Marcos and Adela Pérez. They have come to the bridge after spending the morning trying to fix the broken radio. Lieutenant Thompson nods to them and turns to another police officer standing nearby.

Thompson: Okay, Officer Michaud, get to the other side and see that it's blocked off completely. We've only got a few minutes, so hurry!

Officer Michaud: Yes, sir, Lieutenant, I'm on my way!

Adela: Lieutenant, are we ever glad to see you! I don't think there's much time left.

Thompson: Look, I'm not saying I believe you. Not yet. But those scores are too much of a coincidence for us to take a chance. That's got to be some kind of radio you two have.

Narrator: Before long, River Bridge is cleared of all traffic, and both sides are sealed off. The area below has been emptied of traffic and people as well. Lieutenant Thompson and Marcos and Adela stand to one side and wait.

Marcos: I don't get it. Everyone's out of the way, so if the bridge does collapse, no one can possibly be hurt. And yet the news broadcast said one person was known dead.

Adela: Look! There's your one person. That's a little girl on the bridge!

Marcos: Where? I don't see her.

Adela: Look about 50 yards beyond the toll-booth. She's out on one of the girders!

Thompson: How in the world did she get out there?

Marcos: What time is it?

Thompson: It's 4:59, Pérez. All we can do is hope the bridge doesn't go down.

Marcos: Maybe your watch is fast. Maybe the bridge won't collapse exactly at five o'clock. Maybe the future can be changed. Anyway, we can't stand by and watch a little girl die without trying to do something!

Adela: But, Marcos, how can we—no, Marcos—don't!

Narrator: Even as his wife screams, Marcos breaks away and races for the bridge. He runs across it, heading for the girder the little girl is standing on. Not wanting to frighten her and risk causing her to fall, he stops a few yards away.

Marcos: *(Gently)* Don't be afraid, sweetheart. Just walk to me. No one's going to hurt you. Come on over to me. That's it.

Narrator: Hesitantly, the girl takes tiny steps towards Marcos. Finally, when she comes close enough, he scoops her up in his arms. On the bank, Adela is watching intently.

Adela: Thank goodness! He's got her. But hurry, Marcos, hurry! Get off the bridge!

Narrator: At the very moment Marcos starts his dash for safety, the bridge begins to sway, first slowly, then with increasing movement.

Thompson: *(Shouting to Officer Michaud)* Get ready to grab them! Grab them both! Quick! The bridge is collapsing!

Officer Michaud: I'll do my best, Lieutenant!

Narrator: An awful, screeching noise fills the air, along with the screams of onlookers. Marcos Pérez tries to reach the end of the bridge. But as he nears it, he feels the structure collapsing beneath his feet. He pushes the little girl into the waiting arms of Officer Michaud. Then he tumbles, along with tons of concrete and steel, into the river below.

Twenty miles away, in the town of Lakemore, a woman turns on her radio to listen to her favorite radio station.

Radio Voice: *(Music plays, then...)* I've just been handed a special news bulletin. River Bridge in Somerville has just collapsed. So far, one person is known dead. Stay tuned for more details.

Studying the Elements of a Play

A play is a story that is acted out. Every play has characters, a setting, and a plot. Complete each of the following statements about the play you just read.

Title of the Play _____

Characters are the people or animals in the play.

1. The most important character in the play is _____.

2. Two minor, or less important, characters are _____

    and _____.

Setting tells when and where the events in the play take place.

3. The time (past, present, future) the events in the play take place is

    _____.

4. The place where the events take place is _____

    _____.

Plot is the story the play tells. Plot includes the problem that the main character faces; the main events, or attempts by the main character to solve the problem; and the ending of the play.

5. The problem that the main character faces is _____

    _____

    _____.

6. Two important events, or attempts to solve the problem, are _____

    _____

    _____.

7. The play ends when _____

    _____

    _____.

Think about the characters in the play. When you think about how characters are alike or different, you compare them. Use the chart below to compare two characters in the play. Place the character's initials in the boxes that best describe him or her. You may add more words that describe to the chart. An example is done for you.

Play: _____

Character: _____

Character: _____

	VERY	SOMEWHAT	NEITHER	SOMEWHAT	VERY	
good	A.R.			J.M.		evil
happy						unhappy
careful						clumsy
lucky						unlucky
wise						foolish
friendly						unfriendly
kind						unkind
honest						dishonest
gentle						rough
brave						afraid
proud						ashamed
successful						unsuccessful

Now use a separate sheet of paper to write a paragraph comparing the two characters. Explain how they are alike and how they are different.

Understanding the Characters

The characters in a play do and say things that show what kind of people they are. Select three of the most important characters in the play. Answer the questions about each character you have chosen.

1. Character: _____

   What kind of person is this character? _____

   _____

   _____

   Give an example of something the character did or said in the play that

   supports the description you have given. _____

   _____

   _____

2. Character: _____

   What kind of person is this character? _____

   _____

   _____

   Give an example of something the character did or said in the play that

   supports the description you have given. _____

   _____

   _____

3. Character: _____

   What kind of person is this character? _____

   _____

   _____

   Give an example of something the character did or said in the play that

   supports the description you have given. _____

   _____

   _____

Making a Play Map

Use the play map shown here to tell what happens in the play.

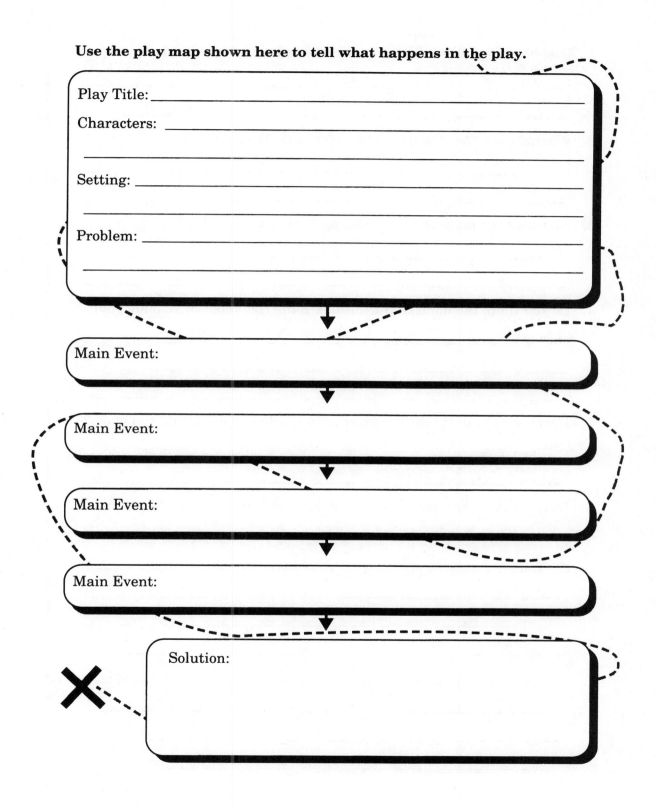

Play Title: _____

Characters: _____

_____

Setting: _____

_____

Problem: _____

_____

Main Event: _____

Main Event: _____

Main Event: _____

Main Event: _____

Solution: _____

Choosing an Alternate Ending

1. Describe the problem that the main character faces in the play.

   _____

   _____

2. What choices does the main character have for solving the problem?

   _____

   _____

3. How does the main character choose to solve the problem?

   _____

   _____

4. Do you think the main character makes the right choice? Explain your
   answer. _____

   _____

   _____

5. If you were in the main character's place, what choice would you make?

   _____

   _____

6. Imagine that the main character makes a different choice. Then write
   a new ending for the play. Use the back of this sheet if you need
   more space. _____

   _____

   _____

   _____

   _____

   _____

   _____